The Ultimate Guide to Legitimate Work at Home Jobs

Over 100+ Well Known Companies

by

Dawn Xhudo

The Ultimate Guide to Legitimate Work at Home Jobs

by Dawn Xhudo

3 Book Special Edition

Dedication

I want to dedicate this book to my husband, Tony. He is the light of my life and without him it just doesn't work. I love you Jerk!

How to Make Money
Get Off Your Ass & Make Some Cash

TABLE OF CONTENTS

1.   YOU CAN DO IT!

2.   LET'S GET ON WITH IT

3.   NOW THAT WE ARE ON THE SUBJECT

4.   WRITING YOUR BOOK

5.   YOU WROTE YOUR BOOK NOW WHAT?

6.   REFERENCES FOR YOUR USE

CHAPTER 1

YOU CAN DO IT!

I did it and you can too. I am not saying go off to work tomorrow and put in your two weeks notice and then run off and rent a secluded cabin to write in. It will take you a bit to get your name out there and your books noticed unless of course you write an over night sensation which from what I hear is like hitting the lottery so be patient. I am just being honest. If you ever wanted to make money without having a job this book will show you how. You don't have to have any experience or go to school for years learning how to write. You can write e-books or articles to sell online and make money on any subject you like. If there is a subject you can think of there is a market for it. Anything from snowboarding in the North Pole to Scuba Diving in the Bahamas. You can count on the fact there is someone out there that does not want to do the research and will buy your e-book or article on the subject because you have already done the research for them. They will purchase your e-book or article simply to gain your expertise on the subject. I have never written a book or published an article in my life until I stumble onto self publishing on Amazon.

I will break down exactly what I have done in easy to follow steps. Right down to including the links to websites that provide free royalty free pictures that you can use not only in your book but on your cover as well. I will include tips and tricks that I used to help you out. My goal is to write these books to help everyone achieve their own personal level of success. My other book "Legitimate Work at Home Jobs & Where to Find Them" was written to help anyone looking for a work at home job find one easily and without being scammed. Nothing boils my blood more than those scammers out there charging people under false pretenses, promising them to make them rich while working at home. Meanwhile all they receive is some email showing them how to scam others out of their hard earned money. Sometimes it is so well written the innocent person looking for work does not even realize that they are scamming someone right away or that they have been scammed themselves. They are so embarrassed about being scammed that 99 percent of the time they do not report it or ask for their money back. This is what the scammers are counting on so they can keep everyone's money.

In this book you will find a totally legitimate way to earn money that you can be proud of. Your friends and family will be impressed, proud and will probably be the first to purchase your books. You can order them yourself and keep a collection of all of your work or you can print and frame the covers of your books to show them off over your desk!

CHAPTER 2

LET'S GET ON WITH IT

The very first thing that you have to do is to figure out what you want to write about. It can be anything. Anything that you might be interested in, anything that you have a vast knowledge of, anything that you think other people will be interested in, etc... If you have always had an interest in say, skydiving, Your friends are referring people to you for advise. You are always talking about it and giving your advise away for free why not write a book? You can then refer everyone to your book and then you will start making money on the subject that you love so much and don't have to give your knowledge away for free.

My husband god love him. He spent years bodybuilding. He has always had a love for physical fitness,
sports, & helping others. Finally he decided to go to school for Holistic Health. Thousands of dollars and years later he found himself giving bodybuilding and health advise away for free to family, friends, friends of family and acquaintances. They were all getting free health and fitness advise. I urged him for years to write books on bodybuilding, sports nutrition & health & fitness. He now has 13 books out and is working on number fourteen on these subjects. He does very well financially and he is no longer giving away his advise for free. When someone asks he simply refers them to his books on the subject they need. Rather than family or friends calling him for help they refer to his books or the best is the word of mouth sales because they are now referring others to his books.

So you see? You can do this too. But it doesn't have to be on a subject that you know very well. It does not have to be on something that you went to school for, for years and spent thousands of dollars on. You can do the research and put it together in an article or e-book yourself. If your e-book is long enough you can sell it as a paperback as well. Amazon has a great self publishing program which allows you to sell your paperbacks as print on demand when someone orders it.
Like I stated earlier I will format this book in easy to follow steps so you can follow them right to your own personal level of success!

Your first step is going to be to sit down and figure out what subject you want to write about and who your target market will be. These people will be the ones to purchase your book. Your job is to market to them. Figure out exactly how to get the word out to these people. I will also point you in the right direction with some tips and pointers on how to do this.

While you are coming up with ideas on the subject you wish to write about you will want to do some research on other books on the same subject. What I do is go on Amazon and other sites who sell books. I look at the best sellers on the subject and see if I can figure out what it is about this book that attracts others to purchasing this book. Is it the writing? The advice given? There is a difference in the writing and the advice given. You can write very well and still say nothing. If you have done research or know how about the subject check to see how on target it is and make notes. I break authors down into 3 categories. 1. Is the book written well but lacks giving the proper info if any is given at all? 2. Then you have some that can't write but have has all the proper info jumbled together lacking any structure. 3. Then finally you will have the authors who can't only write but they have all of the correct info and advice to give.

This is the category that you want to be in.

Check out the cover and see what it looks like. Note what it says, the format, etc.. See if you can figure out what this book has that makes it a best seller. I am not saying to copy someone else's work, I am saying to learn from someone who has accomplished something that is now your goal.
You do not want to put together a complete copy of someone else's work. You do not want to copy their cover, etc. This will open you up to lawsuits which you do not want and kind of defeats the purpose of what we are trying to do here. At the same time you do not want to make an amateurish looking cover either because this will not sell. We will discuss this in the putting together your cover chapter later in the book.

Coming up with the subject of your book should not be hard for you. I am sure you had a subject in mind before you picked up this book. That could be the reason you purchased this book in the first place. Everyone has their own reasons but I would bet that this would be the number one reason for purchasing this book is because most people already have a subject in mind to write about. If not think about it and if you can't come up with something then look up what's hot on the internet and see if anything peeks your interest or could be something that you can write about.

CHAPTER 3

NOW THAT WE ARE ON THE SUBJECT

Now that you have determined what subject you want to write about we can move on. Now comes your target audience. Who are you going to sell your book to? How are you going to get the word about your book out them? Have you even thought about who will buy your book? Well of course this is the most important thing that you will think about when it comes to writing your book. Let's face it this is the main purpose of writing your book isn't it? Hopefully your book will be the means for you to make a lot of money and enable you to be able to quit your day job and write full time.

I will include links to sites that will enable you to market your book for FREE! If you don't have a Facebook page...get one now because Facebook is a very important tool that will enable you to sell many books! I will tell you a little bit more about that later on in the chapter. We will start out with Amazon. This is who I recommend that you use to publish your book. You can use Amazon KDP which is Kindle Direct Publishing. You will earn 35 to 70 percent royalties depending on how much you charge or who buys your book. Now with the program that they have on KDP you can either publish it thru their **KDP Select** which will enable you to give your book as a free promotion for 5 days out of the 90 days that you will be listed as a KDP Select. The program allows you to make money from people borrowing your book. While you are running a free promotion however you do not get paid for your book. This free promotion will get people to notice your book which is the payoff. The more people that know about your book the better. You can try out the KDP and see if it works for you for the first 90 days. While your book is listed as a KDP Select you **CAN NOT** list it on any other forum or sell it anywhere else or Amazon will shut down your listing and cancel your account. So this is a major decision that you need to make. You can get to Amazon KDP thru this link:

https://kdp.amazon.com/self-publishing/signin
openid.assoc_handle=amzn_dtp&openid.claimed_id=http%3A%2F%2Fspecs.openid.n
et%2Fauth%2F2.0%2Fidentifier_select&openid.identity=http%3A%2F%2Fspecs.ope
nid.net%2Fauth%2F2.0%2Fidentifier_select&openid.mode=logout&openid.ns=http%
3A%2F%2Fspecs.openid.net%2Fauth%2F2.0&openid.return_to=https%3A%2F%2Fk
dp.amazon.com%2Fself-publishing%2Fsignin&

If your book is longer than 24 pages you can get it published thru Amazon's **Createspace**. This is a print on demand service. This means that they will publish your book when someone orders it. Createspace is also awesome and I will let you in on a secret. If you are doing an e-book you can start creating your book on Createspace first even if it is not long enough or you just don't want to publish it as a paperback. There is a reason for this which is you can get your ISBN and you can create your cover for free. After you do these two things you can then go to KDP publish your book with your new ISBN and cover. When you have completed publishing your e-book you can delete the started copy from Createspace. Once you create the cover be sure to save it to the computer and open it in the paint program you can then crop it to save a copy of the back and front pages separately. In KDP you will not need the back of the book. Be sure to save it as TIFF or JPEG it has to be at least 1000 pixels on the longest side, with an ideal height/width ratio of 1.6 2500 pixels on the longest side is preferred. You can change the size in the paint program as well so be sure to do this while you are cropping your book cover. Using this trick will save you tons of money creating your cover and there is no need to pay for an ISBN for your book. The only set back is a very small selection of lettering for your book. The god thing is that you have many optional formats for the cover and you can even change the background colors, lettering and pictures. It is possible to make a professional looking cover on Createspace.

Amazon will pay you thru direct deposit right to your account so be sure to put your account info in. You will have to earn at least $10.00 worth of royalties before they will process your direct deposit.

Also be sure to complete an author central page. Make sure you add links to your blog and Facebook page. Once you fill it out you will be able to claim your book which will in turn place your author central bio right on the sale page of your book to enable your potential customers read a bit about your background before purchasing your book.

Another thing that is very important you do is to place tags on your book's sale page. When a potential customer is searching for books on certain subjects they enter keywords into the search bar. Your tags will then include your books in those searches for those specific keywords. This making it a very important thing to NOT forget to do! If you do not ad tags to your book it will still come up but people would literally have to search more in depth to find your book. **LET'S NOT FORGET OUR TAGS!** Once you have the writing bug...start a blog and tell the world about your book. This something that you can start before you even finish your book. Get a buzz going about your book. Use the coming soon angle. I totally recommend **Wordpress**. This blog is awesome and it's free. It also allows you to freshly press your posts which puts them out there allowing people to see them. It also has stats on your dashboard and allows you to use webmaster tools such as **Google Analytics** and **Bing** to see who is reading your blog, how many are reading your blog, which keywords and search engines are used to find your blog. Which of your posts are getting more attention than others. This helps you gauge what is working and what is not so you aren't wasting a bunch of time working on something that your audience is not going to respond to. You also can connect to your **Twitter, Facebook, Pinterest, Tumblr, StumbleUpon, Linkdin, Digg, & Reddit** pages. This will allow your posts to automatically be sent to your pages on these accounts. Whomever your "friended" with on these pages will see these posts. When you post to Facebook you can post to your timeline, your page, to a friend's page or to a group. This is a great feature which gets your posts out to not just your friends or members of your group but to their friends or members as well. Be sure to use Facebook to it's full potential. This will get you tons of traffic to your blog.

On Facebook a group page is another great way to get the word out about your book as I mentioned earlier. Start a group page and allow users to become members of your page. Anyone searching for a subject such as yours will find and join your group. When you post to your group page it will tell you on each post how many people have seen your post. This is a good way to gauge what is working and what is not. Another great feature is ping-o-matic which will update all the search engines with your updated posts. So each time you update your blog with a new post or information go to this site and ping the search engines. Here is the link:

http://pingomatic.com/

Back to Wordpress be sure to use pictures to attract readers. A really good site that I found that has royalty free pictures is Public Domain Pictures. Here is the link:

http://www.publicdomainpictures.net/

This too will save you from spending any money on publishing your book. Because let's face it the reason you are writing your book is probably to make money, right? So why spend when you don't have to.

You can pretty much find any picture that you want of anything that you are looking for to add to your posts or to your books. Very good pictures that are free and they are professionally done as well. I use them on my blog and in all of my books. I have never spent a penny on any of my books. You can use them while doing covers as well. All you have to do is right click on them and save. You can even change the names of them if you want to. I rename them to make them easy to find corresponding to the name or subject of the book I am working on at the time. You can even create separate folders in your pictures to hold the pictures for a certain book this way when you blog and need pictures you can find them easily.
A very important note: Be sure to recognize others blogs. The more attention you pay to their blogs the more attention you will get on yours. Comment often and like their posts. They will reciprocate, I promise. This will mean more attention and more sales!

If you do not already have accounts with **Twitter, Facebook, Pinterest, Tumblr, StumbleUpon, Linkdin, Digg, & Reddit** be sure to sign up with accounts with them to save yourself time later. You will be surprised at how many hits and purchases you will get from these sites. Also be sure to start a list of tags pertaining to the subject of your book ahead of time. You will need them not just for your book but for your posts on your blog and these sites as well.

Here are some links that will enable you to list your books for free to get the word out about your new fantastic book as well!

Remember: If you chose the KDP Select you can't list your book on these sites for sale. I can't tell you this enough. You chose to sell your book exclusively thru Amazon KDP and CAN NOT sell them anywhere else. Even if you think that they will find out. Trust me they will!

The first site that I want to tell you about is **Smashwords**. This site if used properly will allow your book to be listed in it's premium catalog. What this means is that your book(s) will be listed in the Premium Catalog and will be sent out to Amazon, Barnes & Noble, Kobo, Apple, Sony, Library Direct, Baker & Taylor, Baker & Taylor's Axis 360, Page Foundry & Diesel. This is great and it means more exposure for your book(s). They will be listed on all of these websites. Now you can opt out of any of these if you prefer not to sell to one of these companies. You probably will want to opt out of Amazon since you will be more than likely publishing thru them already but if not just do not opt out. On smashwords you can go to the channel manager to make these selections. They have a dashboard to check on the status of your books, your sales, premium catalog status, and books lent out. You can also create coupons for your books as well to give discounts or to run promotions. Smashwords also enables you to create an audiobook of your book to sell thru podiobooks which is a do-it-yourself audiobook publisher.

www.smashwords.com

Podiobooks link:

http://podiobooks.com/

You also can choose to become the publisher of your own books or other's work as well. The publisher setting allows you to choose between your authored books or to change the name of the author to someone else if you desire to do so.

You will need to set up a **paypal** account if you do not already have one or to choose a check option. There is a $10.00 cap for payoff for paypal and a $75.00 cap for a check. Your royalties will need to be atleast $10.00 to get paid thru paypal or you will have to accrue $75.00 worth of royalties to be paid thru check.

The next site is **LULU** this site will also enable you to publish and sell your books. You will have to go thru the publishing process with this site as well. However it is another site to get the word out and to market your book. You will find that each site requires different formats that they will accept you book in such as: .doc, .epub, .pdf, etc... you might want to make a copy of your book in each format. That way you will be ready when you are publishing on each site. I know this sounds like a lot of work but it really is not. If you are not familiar with this all you have to do is go to file at the top of the page click on save as put a 1 or consecutive numbers after the name and below it change the format to what ever you want and save. Very easy stuff. Here is the direct link to LULU:

https://www.lulu.com/account/sign-in

Good Reads is another site that you can use to market your book. However this is my least favorite of them all. You can however add a Goodreads App to your Facebook page and it will show your friends, readers and members what books you are recommending, which ofcourse you can make your books. You can find Goodreads at:

http://www.goodreads.com/

I could go on and on with sites that you can list your books on however this chapter would be never ending. I have listed the most beneficial for your use to get the word out about your book and to sell it. There are also readers who will give free reviews of your book. The more positive reviews and sales you get the more it will move up on the sales rankings and the more apt you will be to be on the best or top sellers list giving you more exposure hence more sales!

Another good way to get the word out about your book is to go onto forums for what ever subject you are writing about and just letting people know about your book. Just don't use overkill or spamming this will just turn people off. Be polite, introduce yourself. Treat it as you are walking up to someone and introducing yourself to them. You wouldn't walk up to someone on a street and push something on them without introducing yourself would you? Of course you wouldn't. So you common courtesy when on forums or anywhere you may have potential customers. I know that it sometimes is easy to lose sight that you are actually talking to a live human being and that what you say in writing can be very easily misinterpreted. Someone can take what you say way, way out of context thru writing. Because your tone of voice and you pronunciation of words do not come thru in writing. Your body language can't be seen thru writing. Unless of course you send a picture or audio clip with it! Just some advice do it however you wish but just please keep this in mind.

CHAPTER 4

WRITING YOUR BOOK

Now that we have covered all of that ground you will are going to start writing your book. Depending on your subject it will be either fiction (something made up) or non-fiction (something that is real). I tend to go for the non-fiction type of writing. I like to write about real life scenarios or real life problems that if I know enough about the subject I will write a book on it if I feel that it will help out my fellow human beings. I will NOT however write on a subject that I know absolutely nothing about and I would suggest that you do not either. Leave that for the professionals of that field. The worst thing you can do id put out incorrect or false information. That will kind of kill your writing career before it even starts. You will probably have to make up a pen name after that one. If there is a subject that is near and dear to your heart and you know a little about it, you want to write on the subject then I would suggest that you do some research and make sure that your facts are straight before you start to write.

Always, always, always and I can't say this enough...**PROOF READ YOUR BOOK BEFORE PUBLISHING**. I have seen so many reviews on indie books and the number one complaint is the spelling, poor use of words, over use of big words and punctuation. People will not buy your books if they are not written properly, put together poorly, your cover looks amateurish and it lacks proper punctuation. Use spell check often. Also if there is a word that I am not sure of the meaning or I want and alternative, I google it.

I have read a million how to get rich writing, or get rich like I did books. As I mentioned earlier this is like hitting the lottery from what I hear. So you must be patient. It does take a lot of hard work and determination. Are there days that I don't feel like blogging? OMG! YES! There are times I don't want to look at my computer at all! But I force myself over and get to work. If you are doing nothing else and you are determined to make it as a self employed published author you will force yourself to do it also. Even my husband who has all of these books under his belt Does he force himself? Yes and when he slack I kick him in the butt to do it as well. We do pretty good for ourselves. Did I quit my day job? NO! I still work and write. One day I hope to quit my day job or retire what ever comes first. Why don't I quit? Because I just do not feel comfortable doing so just yet. But I am sure that I will one day. I do hope that this book helps you to reach what ever goal you are reaching for as well.

Enough of that and onward. Now that you will be writing your new fabulous book you will need a quite place to write. Far, far away from the distractions of the world. There is nothing worse than having something fantastic to say, you get half a sentence down and your interrupted. You go back and read the sentence and can't freakin' remember what that thought was that was so great that you couldn't wait to get it down on paper. So quite place to work is number 1 priority.

You also will want to save your work often as you put it down. I can't tell you how many times either myself or my husband have screamed in horror as we noticed the last 26 pages you just spent days putting down has disappeared into oblivion. You do not want this to happen to you ever. It is a real show stopper. Do you feel like doing all of that work over again? Will you ever remember all of that stuff you wrote that came out so great? NOPE! So please do yourself a favor and take my advice, it takes one second to hit save. Did I just hit save? You bet I did!

While you are writing your book, after you have completed a couple chapters you can create your cover and do a coming soon. You can give people a preview of the first couple chapters of your book to create a buzz before the books is even finished. I would recommend this if you want to get it out there and you can't wait to get feedback.

I also recommend writing down what you want to say on the back cover of your book, the introduction, if you want to do a dedication or anything extra such as marketing material, etc... Also start out with an outline of the information that you want to include in your book. If it will be fiction include your characters, what they look like, any habits they may have, motives, aspirations, who they may like or dislike, what they will get out of something, where they live, how they live, etc... Once you have it down on paper and figure out how you will begin and end your book all you have to do is put it together with your story line. Go back to your notes often as you may forget something that you really wanted to put in.

One thing that I mentioned earlier on was that you want to make sure that you have original material that is all of your own. You do not want to copy anyone else's work. There are sites out there that sell PLR's which are books that they are selling you the rights to. What they don't tell you is that a lot of self publishers recognize these books and will prohibit you from publishing them under your name. Be very careful when buying these books to sell under your name you have to do research on where you are even allowed to sell them and sometimes there are restrictions on if you can even claim them as your own writing. Besides who really wants to publish someone else's work as your own?

You can take however long you wish to write your book. However if you leave it collecting dust and don't work on it you will never make any money on it. I try to write a little each day because if I leave it too long it will start to collect dust, I may let the every day non-sense of life get in the way and I will never finish. What good would that do you? Not much because you would not be reading this right now.

I can't tell you what to write about nor can I write your book for you. I can however point you in the right direction as to self publishing, who I would recommend you use to do this, and where you can get great advertising and marketing for free. If you follow the tips that I have given it is up to you. I have followed these same things and have done pretty good. I can't promise that you will make a million dollars and become famous from writing. I can do what I can to point you in the right direction. So get to writing your book.

CHAPTER 5

YOU WROTE YOUR BOOK NOW WHAT?

Hopefully you have written your book and it did not take too long. Now what you will want to do is to check out the option I have given you in earlier chapters to get your book published. You can go the traditional route if you like. However this is a long, tedious, and drawn out procedure that may never get your book into the hands of readers. Traditional publishers are very picky about what they put out there and really do not want to touch anything that is not going to be a best seller so I would recommend that you work on the self publishing route.

I use Amazon as my self publishing format. You can earn from 35 to 70 percent royalties and they directly deposit the money right into my account. They make it very easy to publish and they give you step by step instructions on how to publish the book. I really don't need to give any tips on how to move forward with this because they have it all covered. No muss no fuss. Awesome is all I can say!

You will need to publish your book thru Createspace and kindle if you wish to sell as a paperback (Createspace) or as an e-book (KDP). Following the earlier chapter if you are going to publish just an e-book be sure to start publishing on Createspace to get your ISBN and your cover created for free. Once you have published your kindle then you can delete the title from your dashboard on Createspace unless you wish to keep and make it longer or if you would like to see how it does as a Kindle and then do it as a paperback later.

Your cover believe it or not sells your book for you. When they say don't judge a book by it's cover, well...most people do. Remember this while designing your book cover. Make sure everything is spelled correctly and do not use amateurish pictures or wording on the cover. Your cover is the first impression of your book. Make it good. This is where the research of top seller's books and what you think may be making them so hot comes into play. I do this with every book I write. I look at books on the same subject that I am writing about and see if I can figure out what makes them appealing to the masses. I don't copy them but I will come up with my own version of this certain thing that I have found. Never copy someone else's work.

If you have not put a title to your book. Do this now. Try to come up with something that you think you would want to see or that you might buy. Something catchy but not corny. This too will attract buyers to your book,

This is where the earlier marketing material info that I gave you comes into play. You will want to start your blog if you haven't done this already. Start a Facebook page if you don't already have one. Once you do that be sure to start a Facebook group on the subject that you are writing about. This will draw readers that are looking for material on the subject or looking for a new good book to read in their genre.

From your blog you can feed your new posts right from your blog to your Facebook time line, group, or page.

You also will want to start a Twitter page to tweet your posts to. Sign up for Digg, Reddit, StumbleUpon, Pinterest, Linkdin, & Tumblr. You can send your posts directly to these pages from your blog. Trust me, much traffic comes from them. The more traffic you get the more sales you will make. Get he buzz going about your book. Also do not be afraid to let people read the first couple chapters or to give out complimentary copies of your work. This too will get your book out there! Word of mouth is the best advertisement for any business venture. This is a business venture so treat as one.

There are literally thousands of self published or affectionately called indie authors out there. We have all traveled down the same path. We all want to be heard, we want people to read and love our books. Think outside the box when it comes to finding your and getting to your target market. If you already are rich and have money, advertise on TV, get a spot on the radio, advertise on billboards. But for the less fortunate of us we have to take the long traveled road of advertising for ourselves. Once you get the book on all of the sites you desire, your blogging about it everyday, try to get yourself a table at a local bookstore and do a book signing. You can also, this is if you are a smooth talker, you can probably get a spot on a talk show to talk about your book. They are always looking for stories and it could be your lucky day. If you could land a spot watch you sales jump! No I have not been so brave as of yet. I just may one day write to Oprah! You can also advertise in magazines or bring your story to the attention of the local Newspaper and see if they are interested in covering a story about a local author in our midst. This too would get you much needed advertising. You can even use **craigslist** to your advantage. Make up an advertisement and post your book under the title on craigslist that you think corresponds to your book. If it is fiction you might want to just post it under books.

Be sure to list your book anywhere you can and don't forget to use your tags. Hopefully you came up with an entire list of them. Also check out other books on a similar subject as yours and check out what tags they used for their book. No problem using the same tag lines as others, you can not get into trouble for this. Think about where you can advertise and don't be afraid to give them away but be sure to ask for reviews. Be sure to talk about your book any chance you get but make sure you are not shoving it down someone's throat. I will not pay to advertise, for reviews, to proofread, to create my cover, or to sell my books. However what ever print on demand publisher you use obviously will be paid for their services thru sales of your book. They will get a cut of your paperback sales and will get a cut of your kindle or e-book sales.

CHAPTER 6

REFERENCES FOR YOUR USE

I am including links to articles, useful material, and info to help you thru the process of coming up with your idea, writing your book, designing your cover, marketing, and selling your book.

http://www.self-pub.net/guides/subsidy.html

http://www.mahalo.com/how-to-self-publish-your-book/

http://www.writing-world.com/publish/selfpub.shtml

http://www.writing-world.com/bookstore/index.shtml

http://www.writers.net/agents.html

http://www.ehow.com/how_6374731_create-book-online.html

http://www.bookemon.com/page/book-making#full-article

http://www.ehow.com/how_2325224_get-book-published-free.html

http://www.ehow.com/how_4470860_self-publish-book-free.html

http://www.ehow.com/video_4974746_write-book-published.html

http://www.ehow.com/how_4793246_book-edited-published.html

http://www.blurb.com/make

http://www.techsnack.net/spotbit-create-free-e-book-online

http://www2.xlibris.com/requestkit8/index.aspx?src=sal&gkw=How+To+Publish+A+

Book

http://www2.xlibris.com/requestkit8/index.aspx?src=sal&gkw=How+To+Publish+A+

Book

http://www.ebookcompiler.com/

http://www.fonerbooks.com/print.htm

There are virtually thousands of references online to help you write and publish your book. I will be including my information and email address at the end of the book if you have any further questions on what to do next. If you get stuck or if you have a simple question to ask or if you just want to give feedback. Everyone is welcome!

How to Make Money
Get Off Your Ass & Make Some Cash

TABLE OF CONTENTS

1. USE POSITIVE THINKING TO GET WHAT YOU WANT

2. A GREAT & FUN WAY TO MAKE MONEY

3. MAKE THE MOST PROFIT

4. EATING YOUR WAY TO PROFIT

5. MONEY MAY GROW ON TREES

6. CASHING IN THE BLING

7. WALK OR SIT YOUR WAY TO RICHES

8. GOT ANY CASH HANDY

9. JACK OF ALL TRADES

10.   PICTURE THIS

11.   BEING A SMART ASS CAN PAY OFF

12. A FEW MORE WAYS TO MAKE SOME CASH

<u>Chapter 1</u>

USE POSITIVE THINKING TO GET WHAT YOU WANT

It really surprises me when people wake up broke, know that they are broke and don't know how they are going to go about making money for what they need. Even if it is a couple dollars to get themselves thru the day. There is an entire world of possibilities out there and all you have to do is go out and get what you need. I don't mean to hit a little old lady over the head and steal her social security check I mean there is a lot of potential and I will help you find the many different ways that you can make money when you really need it.

The first thing they think is "Oh shit I'm broke!" the next thought is "Where am I going to get money?" With those thoughts in mind they don't have a clue as to where to go about getting money because the next thought is "Who can I borrow money from?" This is the wrong direction to go in because you're going to have to pay that money back at some point and if you borrow from some shady character your might end up with your legs broken!

So the first thing you want to do when you wake up broke and ask yourself those questions you should change the last question to "How can I make some money?". Making your own money will make you feel much better about yourself knowing you are not depending on someone else to make it.

I will give you the ideas and all you have to do is run with them. Take them as they are or put your own twist on them. Make them your own. Hopefully by the time you are done reading this you will have the ability to make something out of nothing and have money in your pocket. There are ways to make money all around you.

What it all boils down to is you need to change the way you think. If your lazy and don't want to help yourself then this book is not for you and you will not make money. You will probably quit and then go borrow money from someone. Then you will stay on the same lazy broke path you have been on forever.

But if you are the type of person who legitimately does not know how to the make money that is all around you then you have the potential to open that way of thinking up. We all have potential, we all have a special skill something that you were born with, something that comes naturally to you. Not everybody is able to do what comes naturally to you so you have the ability to use that skill and make money selling it to those of us who were not born with your special skill. There is a market out there for everything. In other words there is someone out there to purchase any thing that you have to market. Why do you think ebay is so successful? There are people out there selling rocks, snips of hair, etc... One guy sold a piece of toast because he said it had come out of the toaster and there was a picture of the Virgin Mary on it. I bet you can search for the stupidest thing you can think of and it will be for sale on ebay. I know I used to sell on ebay and I have put things on there that you would not think would sell and I sold it! No shit! I sold it and it went for a lot more than I thought that it was worth!

Did you ever hear the saying? "One man's trash is another man's treasure? Well that is what I am talking about here. I will show you how to make the money that you need in simple to follow steps. All you have to do is be positive and it will work out for you.

Chapter 2

A GREAT & FUN WAIT TO MAKE MONEY

In this chapter I will start giving you some ideas of how to make money out of what seems like your starting with nothing. Believe me there have been more days than I wish to admit that I woke up broke. More people than not wake up broke. We are the majority and it can be overwhelming, discouraging, and down right degrading to wake up broke. The feelings of desperation take over, you have to admit that the thought of robbing a bank has entered your mind, fantasizing about what it would be like. But then your rational takes over and you know that your not going to rob a bank even though you would like to! My point here is don't let it get you down. Your not going to take it anymore and you are going to make money. Get it in your head! Focus on it and be positive. It will come to you. It is all in the power of positive thinking. If you want it, say it, think it, and know your going to get it. I can not tell you how many times in my life that there were things that I wanted. Did I get everything I ever wanted? Not really, I wish I could say that I have but I can't and I will not tell you that you will get everything you want either. But you can't sit on your couch and expect it to come and knock on your door because that is not going to happen. What you need to do is use positive thoughts that clear your head, look for any step that can you can take to get you closer to your goal and take it. Negativity, procrastination, and fear will not get you there. These are all negative things. It all boils down to you can get what you want if you get the negative out of your mind and life. Negative thoughts cloud your thinking and bring negative things to you. Positive thinking clears you mind so you can think clearly, see opportunity so you can take action to get you closer to your goal!

If you are in need of fast cash like I said earlier most people's first thought would be who can I borrow money from. We are not going to even discuss this because you are not going to do that.

I am a self proclaimed "hustler" not meaning that I hustle people for money. I mean that I hustle to get what I want. I have initiative and drive. I will tell you some of the things that I have done to make money without a job.

My favorite way to make money without a job is to go on Craiglist. I will go one there and look through the free items. There is always something good on there. People that are moving always give away good items. I will contact them, go pick it up, take pictures of it and re-post it for sale! You can even check out the wanted section on craigslist there may be someone looking for what you have just acquired. I have never been stuck with something that I could not sell! This is a great system and it will cost you nothing but time! Usually depending on how good the item is you can probably sell it the same day and there you go you have cash in a day!

I have sold everything from clothes to refrigerators that I got for free on Craigslist!

Another way to make money is to post your own ad on Craigslist that you would like yard sale leftovers, garage and attic items that are not wanted anymore. But you need to specify that you are not a garbage man and that you would like only items that can be reused. There you go you now have a ton of free stuff that you can post and sell. If you have a garage you can put a Yard Sale sign at the end of your drive way and have a Yard Sale every weekend. You can sell the free stuff that you obtained thru your ad and make more money. This is something that I have done. I acquired antiques, furniture, clothes, you name it and made a ton of money on the weekends. I literally would have people knocking on my door when I was not having a sale looking to buy stuff that they had seen at my sale or they were looking for a specific item and wanted to know if I had it. So I had money knocking on my door!

Chapter 3

MAKE THE MOST PROFIT

My next favorite way to make money is to sell old books. Now you don't have to sell old books because I do. You can sell any kind of book you wish to sell. I just happen to have a niche for old books. The most cost effect way to get books to sell is to find out if your local library has a bookstore. They sell all of the books that they take out of their inventory and people donate books to them as well. They usually sell paperbacks for $.50 and hardcovers for $1.00. This leaves it open for a large profit margin if when you sell them. If you get something really good you will make a lot of money on them. I have found autographed books at the library book store! If you can get in good with the people who run the bookstore they will let you pick out of the books that have been donated before they go on the shelf for sale. This will give you the chance to get the really good stuff. If they really like you and you buy a lot of books they may also give you a discount. Leaving some of the books at 100 percent profit when you sell them!

Another good way of getting books is going to yard sales. If you don't see books always ask if they have them. I once went to a yard sale and asked I ended up in a dusty attic. I got 4 boxes of books for $10.00. In those boxes there was one book that I ended up selling on ebay for $600.00. It was an autographed copy of The Last Weekend. Always ask if you don't see any!

You can also put an ad on craigslist asking for books. You may get more responses than you care to pick up.

Now that you have the books where are you going to sell them. Well you can start an ebay seller's account, amazon.com seller account, abebooks.com, biblio.com just to mention a few online sites that let you set up accounts to sell your inventory. You can even put them on craigslist but the other book selling sites are much more effective.

Get to know books, authors, publishers this will give you an advantage when you are purchasing books. You will know their worth. If you have an ipad or kindle you can also take this with you to the bookstore giving you a chance to look the book up and see what it is worth before you purchase it.

I have made a lot of money selling books online. I have sold everything you can think of online. Books have the largest profit margin. They are easy to ship most of the time you can just bubble wrap them and slip them into a manila envelope. If you are shipping a rare book I recommend bubble wrap and a book box. The shipping on books is also very low because of media mail. This keeps your overhead at a minimum.

I also would advise if you are going to sell books to get a book on books & rare books. This will tell you what books are sought after, what publisher's, illustrators, markings, etc... to look for as well as giving you a sample of the author's signature. Anyone can pick up a sharpie and sign a book. Be very careful when dealing with autographed books. Get to know how to tell a first edition because not all first editions state that they are especially the older ones. The more modern books might state that they are first editions. Check the verso (this is the flip side of the title page) this usually will tell you the edition of the book.

Take pictures of the books and when you are describing them in your ad be sure to notate any damage to the book even shelf wear. This will save a lot of trouble later with returns. You can even take pictures of the damage so anyone interested in the book is well aware before they make the purchase. Always be honest! It does not pay in the long run to hide imperfections the person buying the book will see it when it is delivered to them any way. This may cause you to have to refund their money and pay extra shipping charges when you are making the refund.

Chapter 4

EATING YOUR WAY TO PROFIT

I guess by now you know where I am going with this. You can virtually find money anywhere as long as you have the initiative to do so. Like I said earlier if your lazy and expect money to come knocking on your door while you watch a movie or play x-box than you will more than likely be broke for a while to come.

Now on to more ways of generating cash flow. A good way to make money if you like to cook is to offer catering services to friends and family. If you feel really ambitious you can always place an ad offering your services to the public. Just don't bite off more than you can chew at first. I know sometimes offers can arise that are very tempting because of the money that is being offered but you have to be realistic. If you accept the job, take the money and it is more than you can handle it will fall apart. This will cause you all kinds of problems including having to pay back all of that money. This is what we want to avoid. So keep a level head and know what you can handle.

If you really are a "foody" You love to eat and you love to cook you could offer cooking lessons to the less fortunate that do not know how to cook! You can do something you love and make money at it! You can post fliers and do private lessons or find a place where you conduct a full blown class on cooking. You could even break it down to dinners, breakfasts, deserts, etc... offer a class on each one.

If you like to bake do a flier for wedding cakes, birthday cakes, cupcakes, etc. You could bake a bunch of samples of your work and hand them out with a business card or flyer at your local grocery store or mall. Just check with the mall or store first to get the okay to be there. You don't want to go out and not get permission first and then get arrested with your wares in tow. This would just cost you money!

If you don't know how to cook or are an amateur but would love to cook for a living. Get your cookbook out and learn! Find out what you cook the best and specialize in it. There is a market for almost anything out there. Learn your craft. Even professionals are learning something new every day. There is no way that anyone can be the leading authority on something and know absolutely everything there is to know about anyone subject. Work for your dream. There are thousands upon thousands of rags to riches stories out there of people who started their businesses with twenty dollars or less. You just have to be motivated to do so. So put your big boy or girl pants on and let's get to work. Like I said before and will keep drilling this into your head....It is not going to come knocking on your door!

CHAPTER 5

GROWING YOUR PROFIT

My next suggestion for making money would be to advertise your skill for yard work and gardening if you love plants and gardening. You could offer to do anything from trimming hedges to maintaining gardens. You can mow, edge, prune, trim, plant, water, etc. a lot of people do not like to do these things and find them utterly mundane. That's the ticket to making money on things like this. A lot of people do not like to do them and do not want to make the time to do it. The good thing about this kind of work is you can tell by driving past who your potential customers may be. You can target them by putting one of your fliers in a plastic hang bag and hang it off the handle of the mailbox! DO NOT EVER PUT ANYTHING INSIDE A MAILBOX! I can not stress that enough because if you do you may be opening yourself up to tampering with someone's mail which is a federal offense. If you want to be really ambitious you can go door to door and present your flier. This is a bit more direct and you can have a chance to win over your potential customer. You can even offer to do extras such as drive way sealing, gutter cleaning, taking out the trash, shoveling snow in the winter time, cleaning the yard, attic, or garage. Only if you have experience cutting down trees do you offer this service. There are a hoard of dangers both to yourself, someone else or a financial danger if the tree falls on something or someone. So please do not offer to do this unless you have done it before. The same goes for really high gutter cleaning. If you are not experienced in doing this or roof work I would not advise that you offer to do this.

You should also check with the management offices for housing communities in your area. A lot of these places either violate or fine residents that do not mow their grass. You can explain what you do and ask them if it is okay to post some of your fliers for your services.

There are a few things that you may need to own to do this like a lawnmower, shovels, rakes, edger, weed whacker, etc. But there is also the possibility that the people that you are working for may also have these and may let you use them to complete the task. It would be better if you had your own tools just in case you get the job and they do not have their own. What do you do then?

You also may want to read a few books on plants and trees if you plan on pruning, etc... just so you know what time of the year you should be doing this. You do not want to kill someone expensive trees, plants or bushes if you prune them the wrong time of the year. You can also look up a few agricultural websites to get this info. Also use the Farmer's Almanac it can be very useful. The website is:
http://www.farmersalmanac.com/weather/2011/08/29/2012-us-winter-forecast/

CHAPTER 6

CASHING IN THE BLING

There are times when we all find ourselves broke in between paychecks wondering how the heck we will make it until the next payday. Where will you find the money? Well this one is a simple no brainer. You can look around and see what you have in your house that you no longer want or are not using. The fastest way to make money is to look around your home for items that you no longer need or want.

If you have jewelry and want to sell it be very careful and do not sell it to the first person that gives you an offer. Get a couple offers or have your item appraised by someone who is not going to be purchasing your item. The reason I say this is obvious, they may low ball the price just so they can save themselves some money. If you only need a few bucks to get you thru the day and do not want to sell the item you can just pawn the item and then get it back when you have the money. It is like selling it with out selling it and you do not have to pawn it for the entire value. You can pawn it for what ever amount you need. This will make it easier for you to get it back later.

Clean out the attic, garage or storage room. I am sure you will find things that you have forgotten about and have not seen in years. If you have not seen them in years or have not used them I am sure that you do not need them. Why not turn them into something that you do need like money!

Be very careful with any item that may have exceptional value such as jewelry, antiques, rare books, etc... Not everyone is honest and may like I said low ball you to try and buy and save themselves some money. The very same money that you can use.

Like I mentioned earlier you can have a yard sale, put an ad on craigslist, sell it on ebay or pawn it! This will give you enough cash to get thru to your next payday.

CHAPTER 7

WALK OR SIT YOUR WAY TO RICHES

If you have a love for pets, taking care of animals and can't get enough of going to the zoo or shelter than this next tip may just be the thing you need to make some dough.

You can advertise pet sitting or dog walking and walk your way to money. Animal kennels charge up to $100 a day to keep your pet while you are on vacation. This may work to your advantage since the pet owners will not only save themselves money but their beloved pets can stay right in the safety of their own home. All you have to do is make visits there to feed, water and walk. Of course if you are a true lover of pets you will take some time to cuddle, pet and play with them as well.

The best part is that you can do this for more than one family at a time since the pets are staying in their own homes. All you have to do is go from home to home.

You may also be able to offer house sitting services as well. In this day and age no one can ever be too sure of what they are going to come home to when they come back from an extended vacation. You can offer them that peace of mind. You will offer to check on the place, bring in news papers and mail so that it looks like someone is home. You might want to turn on a different light each day or leave a tv on so it looks like someone has been there. This also save the vacationer time because they do not have to call and put newspaper services on hold or have the post office put a hold on their mail while they are away.

With all of this in mind you may be able to make some extra cash by mowing the grass, watering the plants, weeding the garden, washing the cars, etc... The possibilities are endless. Use your imagination and you will make money.

CHAPTER 8

GOT ANY CASH HANDY?

As I mentioned in the earlier chapter for lawn care you could just drive around and see your potential customers. In this chapter we will talk about house care. If you just drive around you can spot the number of homes that are in disrepair. They need painting, roofing, siding, gutters, concrete work, etc.

Under the same principal you could offer these services for a fee. You can do a flier and put it on the mailbox (never inside) or you could use initiative and knock on the door, introduce yourself, and sell your services. Always be sure to look your best while you are doing this. You do not want to knock on the door in disarray. Be sure to have your hair combed, have on clean clothes, and you look your best. When you look your best, you feel your best, and you can sell your best. If they are vacant homes you can go on the tax roll website for that town or county, look up the address and this will tell you who the current owner is. In light of the current foreclosure situation in this company it just may be a bank. You can contact the bank and see if they are interested in your services to keep vandals away from the house. You just may end up with all of their houses to tend to! This also works well with real estate firms that have a bunch of foreclosed homes to get rid of.

You never know some of these jobs could turn into bigger and better things for you. If the homeowner owns more than one home you could possibly get a job taking care of any homes that they have.

Again please do not offer services that you do not know how to do or can not perform. In the end it will make you look bad to the customer and they will not offer you any more work.

Please be sure to check your local and state laws before embarking on any work. There may be licenses or permits needed for certain work.

CHAPTER 9

JACK OF ALL TRADES

In this day there are too many elderly people out there with no care givers. On any given day you can turn on the news and hear about the old man that wandered off and could not find his way back home. The elderly lady who was mugged in an elevator or was found in her filthy home eating cat food because she could not get out to buy real food. With that said there is a large market for people to either sit with the elderly or take them shopping. You could run errands to the store, take them to the doctors or pharmacy. Once you hook up with one elderly person they tell their friends so a lot of your business will be word of mouth. Before you know it you will need a second person to help with all of the things that they need done, This is especially so if you get work in a senior housing development.

They may just want you to take a walk or sit with them. You could get work cleaning their homes, washing their cars (they can no longer drive). Walk their pets. The possibilities are endless. What it boils down to is they have no one to care for them and most of their kids more than likely live far away with families of their own.

This one may entail a little of all of the other job suggestions. They could need repairs done to their homes or cars. Most of the elderly population do not trust anyone coming in to their homes so you may have to earn their trust. Once you get in the door they will tell their friends about you this may lead to more calls for work!

You may find yourself watering their plants, cutting their grass, walking their dogs, painting their homes. Grocery shopping, picking up their medication at the pharmacy, taking them to the doctors, yard work, and taking them to cash their social security checks.

One thing is for sure you will never stop hearing stories of when they worked, went to war, their younger years, how they met, what achievements their kids have made and when the last time they went to bathroom was!

CHAPTER 10

PICTURE THIS

A fun way to make some cash with minimal effort is to take pictures of anything that you can think of. Take pictures of people doing anything you can think of or any kind of animal that you can catch on film. Be sure to get permission if you are taking pictures of people. You can then take those photos and download them. Once you get them downloaded you can start your own website to sell stock photos. There is a great demand for these photos for websites, e-books, regular books, fliers, businesses, etc...

People are willing to pay big bucks for the royalty free photos. This is a fun and great way to earn some cash. You may want to set up a paypal account so you can accept credit card payments on your website if you don't already have one.

While I am on the subject another great way to make money is to write your own e-books. People are always willing to pay for information. You can sell articles on certain subjects or you can sell entire e-books. You will have to know how to market the e-books so you might want to research this before you start your writing career. There is a great demand for e-books.

You can research what the best sellers are before you start to give yourself an idea of what people are looking for. You might even be a great writer and want to write your first novel to sell. I can tell you that romance novels sell like crazy so if you want to go this route it will not do you wrong!

You could also blog. There are a lot of websites out there that will pay you to write articles for them. There are websites that will pay you to do surveys. Google adsense will pay you by click to place their ads on your blog or website and you get paid each time someone clicks on the ad!

You could also become an affiliate to almost any website out there. Place their ads on your site or blog and you get paid when someone either buys something or clicks on the ad.

You can become a freelance writer and offer your services. You can find ads from websites looking for freelance writers.

CHAPTER 11

BEING A SMART ASS CAN PAY OFF!

Did you do good in school? Are you an authority on a certain subject? Do you have a bunch of useless information that you have never needed trapped in your head? If so you can place ads to tutor or teach someone what you know.

Offer classes on the subjects or you can offer hour classes to kids who are getting ready to take a test or need to pass a certain subject in school.

You can also teach classes on what ever subject you are the master of. If you are an extremely good painter you can offer painting classes. If you are a great baker then teach a baking or cooking class. Do you see where I am going with this?

Again use your imagination to create the class you feel most comfortable that you know enough about to teach.

Put up fliers for tutoring or for the class that you want to have. State what the cost will be and request that people email you to register for the class. This way you know how many to expect. Also you can check with your local VFW or anywhere they may have a room that you can use for this class.

Be sure you have all of the materials that you will use for the class ready before that date. Also do your research because you do not want to get up in front of a room of people and not know what you are talking about.

CHAPTER 12

A FEW MORE WAYS TO MAKE CASH

Your opinion really does count so why not make some money giving it. You can take online surveys to make some extra money. Just don't ever pay anyone to give you a job. There are alot of scam artists out there today so if anyone asks you to give them money to give you a job tell them no thanks and move on.

There are alot of businesses out there that will pay for your opinion. You can check out the nearest companies to you that will pay you to be part of a focus group. All you have to do is sit in a room with other people and talk about what you think on a certain subject or product.

You can donate blood or sperm for cash. You can sell your eggs and there are people that will also buy your hair to make wigs. Like I said earlier there is a market for just about anything. There are people selling pieces of toast and rocks on ebay for heaven's sake so if you have a service or a product there is a market out there for it. Don't ever let that last question be

"Who can I borrow money from." Have some initiative and make some money on your own. Be independent go out and get what you want in life and never ask anyone for anything again.

If you are looking for a work at home job I am going to say it again.....DON'T EVER PAY ANYONE TO GIVE YOU A JOB!!!! You can find hundreds of companies that are looking to hire people to work at home. It works out great for the companies because they do not have to pay the overhead to have on site employees. Most of the jobs are for independent contractors so they do not have to pay over time, vacation pay, sick pay, etc...For more info on this subject you please read on to the next section. This is where you will find Legitimate Work at Home Jobs & Where to Find Them.

It lists over 100 legitimate companies that are looking to hire people to work at home!

Legitimate Work at Home Jobs & Where to Find Them

TABLE OF CONTENTS

1. THE WORK AT HOME BULLSHIT ARTISTS

2. ABOUT THE REAL LIVE COMPANIES THAT HIRE

3. HOW TO GET THE COVETED AT HOME POSITION

4. KNOW THE COMPANY BEFORE THE INTERVIEW

5. YOU MADE IT TO THE INTERVIEW

6. HELPFUL LINKS, WEBSITES, & OTHER RESOURCES

7. THE HOLY GRAIL REAL WORK AT HOME COMPANIES!

8. NOW GO GET THAT JOB!

STOP AND READ THIS!!!!!!!!!!
TIRED OF THE "WORK AT HOME" BULLSHIT SCAMS?

THIS BOOK WILL GIVE YOU LEGITIMATE COMPANIES THAT REALLY DO HIRE PEOPLE TO WORK FROM HOME. YOU WON'T BE MAKING BRACELETS, STUFFING ENVELOPES, OR SCAMMING SOMEONE ELSE TO GET THE MONEY BACK THAT YOU PAID TO GET SUDDENLY RICH. NO YOU WON'T BE SUDDENLY RICH FROM THIS BOOK. YOU MIGHT MAKE $12.00-$15.00 AN HOUR BUT YOU WON'T GET RICH! I HAVE WORKED AT HOME FOR LEGITIMATE COMPANIES THAT PAID ME PRETTY GOOD WAGES AN HOUR. DID I GET RICH? NO, I HAD A REAL JOB BUT I DIDN'T GET RICH.

YOU DO HAVE TO CONTACT THE COMPANIES, INTERVIEW WITH THEM ON THE PHONE, SOME IN PERSON. BUT IT IS A REAL LIVE JOB IN THIS ECONOMY
IF YOU ARE NOT SERIOUS ABOUT LOOKING FOR WORK THEN DON'T BUY THIS BOOK. YOU WILL HAVE TO DO THE LEG WORK TO GET THE JOB JUST LIKE WHEN YOU ANSWER AN AD FOR A POSITION. ONCE YOU GET THE JOB YOU CAN SIT HOME IN YOUR PAJAMAS AND SLIPPERS TO DO THE WORK BECAUSE NO ONE WILL SEE YOU.

CHAPTER 1

THE WORK AT HOME BULLSHIT ARTISTS

Are you tired of looking for a real work at home job. Well let's face it 99 percent of the time those work at home scams (yes, that is what we will call them) Will only cost you money and leave you wondering how you ever fell for it.

Go ahead and search "work at home". What did you come up with?

I will tell you right now you are probably looking at a screen full of pages promising that you will become rich in hours if you follow the same simple steps that the owner of the web page followed.

There is probably a picture of some older guy (wearing a suit) with a big fat smile, standing in front of a red Ferrari & a mansion with some young chick on his arm (wearing a bikini no less). Because it makes so much sense that he is wearing a suit and she is in a bikini, right?

He got rich, got a re Ferrari, a mansion and a young chick in a bikini this way. So why can't you? BULLSHIT! Then he will go on to tell you that he is only offering this for a very limited time so you better act quick! His friends are all telling him he nuts for giving away his knowledge for such an unbelievably low price!!! But he is such a good guy he wants to help you get what he has. So all you have to do is take the last $34.95 in your bank account or go into overdraft to pay him. After you pay him your hard earned cash he will then give you the knowledge you need to become RICH like him!!!!

Don't worry about the last $34.95 or the overdraft because you will be rich like him in a few short hours!
They didn't get rich by some unknown secret. Come on let's face it. They got rich from this brilliant website ripping people like us off!

The only secret there is, is that you will get nothing for your money. He will send you information on how to set up a website just like his so you can rip people off too!!!!! That is truly what we all aspire to be right? A bunch of rip off artists,
What they bank on is that people will just chalk it up to "Oh well at least I tried" and never ask for a refund. Most of the time because they are embarrassed that they fell for it and to ask for a refund. This is how these people scam you and they are the only ones getting rich!

Please do me and yourself a favor. The next time you a ready to press that cash out button....open up another search screen. Type in the name of the person or the name of the fantastic program that they are trying to sell you and follow it up with the word "scam", press enter and see the number of poor hard working people that came before you that were scammed by these predators. You may be surprised and very thankful that you took the time to do so. This just saved you from making a big mistake, the time it will take trying to get your money back, your dignity and most important of all the $34.95 or the overdraft fee! **DON'T EVER PAY ANYONE FOR A JOB!!! NOW DOES THAT MAKE SENSE?**

CHAPTER 2

ABOUT THE REAL LIVE COMPANIES THAT HIRE

I will provide you with a list of real live companies. Some of which I am sure that you have heard of before that are looking for people to work at home. You do have to work. You probably will be an *independent contractor* meaning that you will be responsible for paying your own taxes and own office related expenses (internet, computer, office supplies, etc...). Keep your receipts because at tax time you can write this stuff off, You will probably be paid thru direct deposit. Every company is different in the rates and way they will pay you. Most pay direct deposit. This is something to find out directly from the company.

Jobs online at not easy to find. That is why I have done all of the leg work to find the best companies that offer real jobs to work from home at.

There is currently a trend of hundreds of companies that offer you to stay at home and do the work they need done. Since you will be an independent contractor they will not have to pay you overtime, benefits, the cost of your electricity, buying computers (you must have your own), IT to fix it, etc. The possibilities are endless saving them money while offering you a job!

I will also offer you a list of forums (which will require you to register) They are great to get info, make some friends and get information on the companies that you are interested in approaching for the job!

The best part of working from home is you don't need a babysitter (which is great for young mother's, single mom's or dad's, young families that can't afford for the wife to work because child care is so dang expensive) You won't have to pay commuting fees like tolls, gas (that's a big one!) insurance, shoot you don't even have to have a car if you don't want one! Your schedule is usually flexible. You can usually work around Dr's appts, shopping, everyday tasks you need to get done.

You don't have to worry about Nosy Nellie from the office always wanting to know what your up to. Irritating bosses looking over your shoulder and seeing that you popped on to check your email that 1 minute out of the day. You don't have to worry about Norbert from IT stealing your lunch from the company refrigerator in the break room while you were at your desk.

It doesn't matter if you did your hair that morning or put on make up. You don't have to spend all night doing laundry because you have nothing to wear to work the next day. If you have a nose peircing, or tatoo on your face....doesn't matter!!!! NO ONE IS GOING TO SEE YOU!!!!!

As an independent contractor you set your hours! Yes you do. Look up and know your rights as an independent contractor. You schedule your hours!

If you are actually hired by the company as an employee then the rules do change. You need to work when they tell you to work. Pretty much like a job that you have to go to every day. In this case they may offer you benefits, vacation, or sick days.

Home based work works out so much better for companies and the home based worker. Say for instance your child is sick and you had to go out to go to work. You are more apt to call in because your little one is sick. Home based work you probably won't call in, you probably will work that day!

You will get breaks, lunches, etc....

You do have to remember even tho you are working from home you will need a quiet place to work and will need the ability to shut off whatever is going on in the rest of the house. You might want to consider a room with a door that you can lock. Don't get me wrong there will be distractions by the tons depending on where you live. Especially if your best friend Sue is used to the unemployed you and comes to visit every day at 2pm not matter what. You will have ringing doorbells, fighting neighbors, phones ringing, cat scratching at the door, etc... TUNE IT OUT!!!!!!!!!!!!!!!!

CHAPTER 3

HOW TO GET THE COVETED AT HOME POSITION

A Little Advice

You have to be on point and on your toes when it comes to interviewing with these companies. There are jobs and for those jobs there are plenty of applicants. I am not in any way trying to disappoint you or keep you from seeking employment with these companies. I am just trying to give you a heads up so you have a better chance of getting the job over someone who is not aware of the competition. With that said these companies have the leisure of being picky. So I am going to spit on my forefinger and wipe off your cheek here. If my advice is to work for you, the better you will do, meaning you will win that at home job! **Remember the competition!** Be on point, be ready for your interview, find out about the company thru research. You will want to come across as professional, that you know what you are looking for, you know your line of work, be confident, know what kind of computer, internet access you have, etc....

Your Resume

Make sure you have an updated version of your resume. That it is one page so the interviewer can scan right thru it and see your qualifications. Add references or you can simply state at the very bottom that they are available upon request as I do. It only takes up too much space the other way. Make sure you include previous employment history with dates, supervisor's name, address and a working number to get to them, Your objective be very specific with this. Bullet each of your skills under your objective making it easy for the interviewer to see your qualifications, and your education. Any special hobbies that you have that are related that is...make sure you include them. Be enthusiastic!!! Companies love upbeat people as opposed to someone who is going to sit on their hands shrugging their shoulders. My last suggestion is very important. I know the competition is stiff. I know it is very easy to do. BUT PLEASE DO YOURSELF A FAVOR AND DO NOT LIE!!!!

A lot of people tend to tell little white lies on their resumes. I currently work in the property management field and run a military housing site today. Which means that I have to weed thru hundreds of resumes when we have a position to fill. Lying on your resumes WILL come out. Whether it is before your hired or even worse after you are hired. If it comes out after your are hired...more than likely you will lose your job for lying on your application. So make me proud, companies will respect you more for telling the truth. I will give you a for instance (keeping my characters fictional) If I had a position available and the person lied about their qualifications and they were hired. It will be very apparent to me that they lied on their application about their skills the first time they were asked to carry out the task that was bulleted as a "special skill on their resume and could not do it. That person would eventually lose their job. Why? Because they lied about their skills. SO I CAN'T SAY IT ENOUGH.......PLEASE DO NOT LIE ON YOUR RESUME! Make me happy and keep your job!

MAKE SURE DURING YOUR INTERVIEW YOU ARE

PROFESSIONAL, TAKE A BREAK AND LET THE INTERVIEWER SPEAK. BE QUICK WITTED, SHOWCASE YOUR SKILLS, AND BE CONFIDENT!

CHAPTER 4

KNOW THE COMPANY BEFORE THE INTERVIEW

Do Your Research

Once you pin point the company or companies (I suggest picking a few) do your research on the company. Find out who started the company, what the circumstances were around it, how fast the company grew or is growing. This will also help you to know how stable your position will be. Go on the blogs, forums, etc...for that company and find out what you can. You might even meet some people that can aide in your job search this way. Find out if there are any interesting stories behind the company. Know who the CEO is, who your boss may potentially be, who his or her boss, know the product. Once you know the product look into the specifics about the product. What is it used for, how does it work, how did it come to be, where is it going in the market, etc....

Listen to What the Ad Says Please

Read the ad for the position. If it says to please send your resume thru email in .doc format. Please do so. If it states to fax it then fax it along with your cover letter. If it asks for salary requirements, then send it included in your cover letter. THIS IS VERY IMPORTANT AND PLEASE LISTEN TO ME ON THIS ONE. If the ad states NO PHONE CALLS PLEASE.........THEN DON'T CALL!!! This is a big pet peeve of mine. If I place an ad and state no phone calls and someone calls. I will intentionally not call that person in for an interview or they will be placed at the very bottom of the stack. Do you know why? Yes, they did not follow direction. So what do you think they will do if I hire them? You got it...NOT FOLLOW DIRECTION. Again so please do not call if the ad states do not call!

Know What You Will Need to Work at Home

Computers are an essential part of working at home, along with your phone and your fax machine. There may be other things that you will need to have to do the job please learn what they are and know how to use them before you are hired. Also make sure that your internet security is up to date and working. No company wants their info our there and at risk of being stolen or used in a malicious way.

Don't Be Disappointed if You Don't Hear Right Away

As I stated before these companies get a ton of resumes for open positions. Be patient. You can check out the blogs and the forums to see if there is any updated news on their open positions. It may take little bit for them to get back to you. They may call you or email you. Check your messages a couple times a day to see if you have gotten a response. You don't want to leave these messages sitting in your inbox for a couple days or a week. When you finally get a response be yourself, showcase your skills, be confident and yes even over the phone smile. That smile will come thru in your voice!

CHAPTER 5

YOU MADE IT TO THE INTERVIEW

Good for you! I am so proud of you for making it this far! Don't be nervous and remember what I told you. Be Confident, be yourself, be enthusiastic, showcase your skills, know the company, and DON'T LIE!

Prepare For Your Interview

Make sure you set up an interview for a time that no one will be around or have somewhere you can go so there is no background noise, or interruptions. Hopefully you have already set up a home office in anticipation of getting a home based job. If the interviewer hears your dog barking, you little one pulling on your leg asking for you to fill up his sippy cup, etc....this would be good cause for you to NOT get the job. This is one of the main reason that you would flunk your interview.

From my own personal experience being interviewed by at home companies the interview should take around 20 minutes or so. Make sure you take a breath while speaking just to give the interviewer time to chime in. Do not take over the conversation! But don't be silent either. Answer the questions being asked. Elaborate when needed.

Make sure you make notes and have them available to glance at while you are on the interview. This is a great advantage that you have for a home based over the phone interview. You can have your resume in front of you, notes that highlight your accomplishments, the notes from the research for the company, your dates, address, and phone numbers for previous employment, references names, addresses and phone numbers. This should make you feel better than a face to face interview. You can even stick out your tongue at your interviewer (I suggest a smile) and they will never know. Unless of course you are Skyping the interview. Make sure you have something to write with to jot down notes or points that you want to remember.

Always be prepared for the staple interview questions. Like "Why do you feel this position is right for you?" or "How can you benefit the company?" Those kinds of questions. They are brutal and nine times out of ten, catch you off guard shrugging your shoulders. Take the time to sit down do an internet search on "interview questions", write them down and come up with the best answers you can come up with. Have them available at your interview. This again is an advantage of having phone interviews!

Be Prepared

Make sure you know who you are going to interview with, their name, their position, contact info is crucial incase you need to make contact later. It is okay to call back later and state that you had interviewed and that you had a further question(s) that you did not think of during the interview. You can even ask during the interview if it is okay to call back later if you have further questions or concerns.

Shut the Hell Up for a Minute!

As I stated earlier pace yourself giving the interviewer time to interject, state something, or ask a question. No one likes someone talking over or interrupting them. This is the wrong time to do this and this is the wrong person to do it to if you want the job. If you know you have a problem with this then try to practice pacing yourself in your at home conversations. Before you know it you have learned the art of effective listening. Plus you won't have people getting mad at you. I had a huge problem with this not because I was rude but because I always have so much to say. I had to learn to pace myself
giving others a chance to speak. You will be surprised at what you will now learn because before you were concentrating on what you were going to say next rather than listening to what the other party was trying to tell you. So pace yourself.

Now That You Have Learned to Listen to Others

Now that you are listening rather than thinking of what to say next. You have your pen and paper handy. While the other person is speaking jot down key phrases that they are saying and para-phrase when you have a chance to speak. This is called the "mirroring technique" This will impress the interviewer because it shows them that you were intently listening to what they were saying. This will also help you to not give simple minded yes or no answers. Try to ask what you want to know in open ended questions. Meaning the interviewer will have no choice bit to answer with information themselves. They too will not be able to give you a simple minded yes or no answer. Plus they could end up giving you important information in those answers that you can use.

After The Interview it is Totally Acceptable to

Send the interviewer a thank you email. Thank them for taking the time out of their busy day to interview you. Thank them for choosing you as one of the candidates for the job. State that you know they get many resumes. That you feel privileged to have been picked out of many and that you look forward to hearing from them in the near future.

NOW ALL THERE IS LEFT TO DO IS WAIT PATIENTLY FOR A RESPONSE.....CHECK YOUR MESSAGES ON YOUR PHONE AND EMAIL

FREQUENTLY.

CHAPTER 6

HELPFUL LINKS, WEBSITES, & OTHER RESOURCES

There are several sites that may be very helpful in your research & job search. Here are just a few that I have found very helpful.

Helpful Links
http://www.internetbasedmoms.com
http://www.work-at-home-forum.com
http://www.whydowork.com/forums/
http://www.work-at-home-forum.com/
http://www.workathomecompanies.net/custservice.html
http://www.saching.com/Home-Based-Customer-Service-Agent.htm
http://www.focus.com/fyi/10-best-and-10-worst-companies-customerservice/
http://www.ehow.com/how_5658291_companies-based-customer-serviceagents.html
http://www.simplyhired.com/
http://telecommutingusa.com/?
redir=frame&uid=telecommutingusa4ff0e105e07e41.83495564
http://www.telecomcareers.net/
http://www.linkup.com/
put in your search word telecommute or telecommuting

Like I stated before you may have to register to use these sites but they are very helpful and you may meet some new people that can either point you in the right direction or aide in your job search.

These sites will also give you the most up to date info available on the companies that are looking for people to work at home.
They will also give you the general requirements for the job.

Remember-check out the company, do your scam search, DON'T EVER PAY ANYONE TO GIVE YOU A JOB! This is so does not make sense. Why in the world are you looking for a job in the first place? To make money right? So why on earth would you pay someone to give you a job? Think about it. But yet everyday people are paying someone because they think they either they will get rich from it, or will get a job out of it. What happens? They end up broker than they were before they started. So please DO NOT EVER PAY ANYONE TO GIVE YOU A JOB!!!! I can not say it enough!

CHAPTER 7

THE HOLY GRAIL REAL WORK AT HOME COMPANIES!

Here is a list that I have compiled of legitimate companies looking for people to work at home in the Customer Service Field. As I said before do your homework. Check out any company that you apply for expecially if you do not recognize the name.

Customer Service Jobs

1800Flowers- http://ww30.1800flowers.com/template.do? id=template8&page=9000

1-800-Contacts- http://1800contacts.iapplicants.com/searchjobs.php

1-800-Translate- http://www.1-800-translate.com/Careers.php

AAA (American Automobile Association) - http://workathomemomrevolution.com/customer-service-jobs/aaa-hiringwork-at-home-customer-service/

ACC Direct- http://www.acddirect.com/jobs/

Alpine Access- https://www.alpineaccess.com/index.php/

Live OPS- http://www.liveops.com/ Working Solutions- http://www.workingsolutions.com/

Arise- http://www.arise.com/

CustomLoyal- http://www.customloyal.com/contact_us.html

Accenture http://careers.accenture.com/usen/working/overview/environment/Pages/index.aspx

Accolade- http://www.accoladesupport.com/techjob.html

AT&T- http://att.jobs/

Accutran Global- http://accutranglobal.com/

Admissions Consultant- http://www.admissionsconsultants.com/employment.asp

Advanis- http://www.advanis.ca/Corporate/CareersAdvanis

Aetna- http://www.aetna.com/about-aetna-insurance/aetna-careers/find-acareer/index.html

Amazon- http://www.amazon.com/gp/help/customer/display.html? nodeId=200692640&view-type=stand-alone

Aura Log- http://www.tellmemore.com/about/aboutus/careers/

Convergys- http://careers.convergysworkathome.com/

VIP Desk- http://www.vipdesk.com/info/careers/

West at Home- http://www.westathome.com/

Teletech- http://www.hirepoint.com/

Telereach- http://www.telereach.com/

ARO- http://www.callcenteroptions.com/

Transcom- https://www.cloud10corp.com/

Ecallogy http://www.ecallogy.com/careers.html

GE (General Electric)- http://www.gecallcentercareers.com/search.asp

GE has their very own Blog pages: http://www.grcblog.com/ http://www.bloggingnext.com/ http://www.edisonsdesk.com http://www.fromedisonsdesk.com

O'ccurance Teleservices- http://www.istayhome.com/

SCI At Home- http://sciathome.com/index.htm

SCM (Secure Call Management)- http://www.securecallmanagement.com/careers.htm

Blue Cross Blue Shield- https://www.bcbst.com/about/careers/openings/

Service 800-- work-at-home-job

Time Communications-

http://www.timecommunications.biz/company/employment
Voice Log- http://www.voicelog.com/
Office Depot- http://www.officedepot.jobs/
American Express- http://careers.americanexpress.com/
CCI (Call Center International)- http://www.ccicompany.us/
Cox Communications- http://ww2.cox.com/aboutus/careers.cox
Cruise.com- http://www.cruise.com/cruise-information/employment.asp? skin
Denihan Hospitality Group -
https://www.ultirecruit.com/man1003/jobboard/ListJobs.aspx? __VT=ExtCan
Enterprise- http://careers.enterprise.com/
Hilton Worldwide- http://hrccjobs.com/
HSN (Home Shopping Network)- http://www.hsn.com/hsn-careers-workfrom-home_at-4983_xa.aspx?nolnav=1
J. Lodge- http://www.jlodge.com/careers/
JetBlue- http://www.jetblue.com/work-here/
Kelly Services -
http://www.kellyworkathome.com/web/us/customers/kellyathome/en/pages/home.html
Express Scripts -
https://www.medcohealth.apply2jobs.com/ProfExt/index.cfm?
 fuseaction=mExternal.showSearchInterface
Sitel- http://www.sitel.com/index.php?p=Careers&pageId=7

Data Entry Jobs
Axion Data- http://www.axiondata.com/
Diondata Solutions- http://www.diondatasolutions.net/opportunities.htm
Key For Cash- https://www.keyforcash.com/
Capitol Typing- http://www.capitaltyping.com/
Caption Colorado- http://www.captioncolorado.com/employment
Speak Write- http://typist.youdictate.com/TypistNav/Employment/index.cfm

Bookeeping
Balance Your Books- http://www.balanceyourbooks.com/
Bookminders- http://www.bookminders.com/?page_id=176

Telemarketing
Custom Loyal- http://customloyal.com/employment
Intelemark- http://www.intelemark.com/
Rich Enterprises- http://www.richworldwide.com/careers.htm
Optum Insight- http://www.axolotl.com/careers.html

Transcription
eTranscriptionist- http://www.verbalink.com/
MedQuist- http://mmodal.com/
MT Recruiters- http://www.mtrecruiters.com/
Production Transcripts- http://www.productiontranscripts.com/jobs.php
SpectraMedi- http://www.spectramedi.com/jobopening.htm
Talk2Type- http://www.talk2type.net/transcriber.html
Tiger Fish- http://www.tigerfish.com/employment.html

Trandscend- http://www.transcendservices.com/
Transcription 2000- http://www.transcription-services.org/requestemployment.php
WenMedX- http://www.flexjobs.com/jobs/telecommuting-jobs-at-webmedx
CHMB- http://www.chmbinc.com/about/careers/
TCN- http://www.codingnetwork.com/medical-coding-jobs/
Coding Compliance Management-http://www.ccmpro.net/Career_Opportunities.html
Eight Crossings- http://www.eightcrossings.com/career.php
Medifax- http://medifax.net/employment.htm

Writing
About.com- http://beaguide.about.com/
Write For Cash- http://www.writeforcash.com/
Write Jobs- http://www.writejobs.com/jobs/
Sun Oasis- http://www.sunoasis.com/
Allvoices- http://www.allvoices.com/incentive
Aria- http://www.ariacallsandcards.com/positions/writejob2.htm
Demand Media Studios- http://www.demandstudios.com/
Families.com- http://about.families.com/become-a-blogger
Quicktate- http://typists.quicktate.com/transcribers/signup
Smart Brief- http://corp.smartbrief.com/about/careers.jsp

Misc Jobs
At Home Signing- http://www.athomesignings.com/signingagents.htm
Compbiz- http://compbiz.net/default.aspx?
Delta Document Services- http://www.deltadocument.com/
Pioneer Staffing- http://www.pioneerstaffing.com/
Sun Lark Research- http://sunlarkresearch.com/Work-for-Us.php
Team Double Click- http://www.teamdoubleclick.com/
Virtual Office Temps- http://www.virtualassistantjobs.com/jobs.html
Elance- https://www.elance.com/
Freelancer- http://www.freelancer.com/
ChaCha- http://about.chacha.com/about/careers/
Staffcentrix- http://www.staffcentrix.com/
Odesk- https://www.odesk.com/o/profiles/browse/
Aim for A Tutoring- http://www.aim4a.com/tutors.php
Art & Logic- http://www.artlogic.com/careers/
Bi Lingual America- http://bilingualamerica.com/main/error/404?
code=404&uri=%2Fmain%2Fcareers.htm
Cape Shore - http://wholesale.cape
shore.com/members/login_about_us.php?
page_id=13&PHPSESSID=2c807034f7802145d86cf404427f765e
Click Accounts- http://www.clickaccounts.com/whoweare_careers.html
Conifer Health Solutions- http://www.coniferhealth.com/careers.html
ejury.com- http://www.ejury.com/jurors_signup.html
Jury Test - http://www.jurytest.com/index.cfm?action
Mandiant- http://newton.newtonsoftware.com/career/CareerHome.action?
clientId=4028f88c274d9c0b01274e8f98e70141
Patch- http://www.patch.com/jobs Perkett PR- http://www.perkettpr.com/careers.htm

CHAPTER 8

NOW GO GET THAT JOB!

Now that you have literally over a hundred places to look for an at home job the possibilities are endless.

Please remember your attitude is everything. Make sure your resume is up to date and condensed. Keep it clean and precise. Do not lie on it, always tell the truth. Do your research on what ever companies you are applying for.

Getting Paid

Be sure to check out what the company is offering you. Some pay by the minute, hour, or by the amount of work. Always make sure you know what you will be getting and when you will be paid. Almost all of these places since they are telecommute jobs will pay you thru direct deposit so you have to have a checking or savings account. I do believe that there are pre-paid cards that accept direct deposit now. So check them out if you do not want a bank account.

Work is Work

Set up your home office so you will not be distracted while you are working. Be sure that your kids know that you are working and can not be interrupted. Make sure there is a door that can stay shut.

Independent Contractors

Odds are you will be an independent contractor. If this is the case you will be responsible for your own taxes, upkeep, computer equipment, office supplies, travel expenses, etc.... Keep all of your receipts since you can write this all off as a business expense. Also since you are an independent contractor this opens you up to telecommute for more than one company at a time! You are basically your own boss and it is like owning your own business! Please look up the laws on the Department of Labor Website so you know what your rights are as an independent contractor.

Testing by the Company

Be prepared for a multitude of tests the company may ask you to take. There are typing tests, voice auditions, math tests, etc.... The list goes on and on. This should be outlined in the job advertisement. If not when they make contact they will let you know what kind of testing they will require you to take.

Know Your Office Equipment Before the Call

Be sure you know your computer make, speed, and capabilities. Your fax machine, internet speed, calculators, phone lines, who your carrier is, etc..... They will ask!

Be Professional

Always present yourself as a professional. Smile even though no one can see you over the phone. This will project into your voice. Be enthusiastic, upbeat and happy. While interviewing make sure you pace yourself giving the interviewer time to speak themselves.

NOW THAT YOUR ARMED WITH ALL OF THIS IMFORMATION....GO OUT AND GET 'EM!

dawn.xhudo@yahoo.com

If interested you can also check out my blog I list free work at home job postings and am sure not to post scams. The link is:
http://noscamsworkathomejobs.wordpress.com/

The link for my Facebook group is:

http://www.facebook.com/groups/264125103700661/

www.ingramcontent.com/pod-product-compliance
Lightning Source LLC
Chambersburg PA
CBHW041114180526
45172CB00001B/248